CHICKAMAUGA, CHATTANOOGA, GRANGER, GRANT, and GRANDPA

By

June Irene Anderson

In the spirit of Henry Annes

June Anderson

ISBN: 0-75962-648-0

This book is printed on acid free paper.

1stBooks - rev. 6/26/01

DEDICATION

This is for the Annis girls—Lucerne, Doris, my mother Lois—my sisters and cousins, their children and mine.

ACKNOWLEDGEMENTS

Although it helps to be a hermit when one is researching and writing a paper of this length, there are still many people and institutions whose help makes such a work possible. I'd like to thank my daughter, Terri Thompson, for granting me temporary possession of her wonderful electric typewriter even though she had papers of her own to write. I must also tender appreciation to the rest of my family for sharing their wife, mother, and kitchen table with that very same typewriter for the duration. I am especially indebted to Dr. Susan Bowers whose encouragement, support, and expertise enabled me to accomplish this project, and the College of St. Catherine for providing me with the opportunity to realize my goal.

PREFACE

As sometimes happens when one is looking for a particular item, she chances upon something of greater value or interest. So it was with me several years ago when I was busily tracking down my ancestors. The Annis family seemed to be a good branch of the family tree to explore, for its roots go deep into American history and are well documented. Apparently Cormac, born in Enniskellen, Ireland in 1638, was the first one off the boat, for a Historical and Biographical Sketch of the Annis Family compiled by the U.S. Research Bureau located him in Newbury, Massachusetts in 1666 where he took Sarah Chase as his wife on May 15th. During the next one hundred years the Annis family prospered and multiplied. Several of that number attended the Boston Tea Party and at least ten fought in the Revolutionary War.

Succeeding generations of Annises produced Abraham in 1674, John in 1700, Jacob in 1741, his son Jacob in 1769 who was the father of Charles, born in 1794, who was the father of Henry, born in 1831, which brings me full circle and back to the purpose of this narrative. Henry Brown Annis was my mother, Lois Annis's, grandfather, and Mother had, as her legacy, a copy of his Civil War Memoirs.

The title on the first of the forty-nine handwritten pages identified the manuscript as "Our Experience At and On Lookout Mountain, November 24, 1863." I eagerly set to work making a typewritten copy of the hard-to-read pages, hoping to find out what my newly discovered ancestor had experienced on that mountain. This was not an easy task, for time had faded parts of the ancient copy into oblivion, and more current events had crowded out knowledge of that portion of our history.

The first problem was easily solved when Aunt Lucerne, keeper of the original diary, sent me a fresh, readable copy. But I was still faced with the question: What is this all about? Then, while browsing through the "F" section of the Reference Library at the College of St. Catherine, I made a discovery that, to quote Henry Annis, "made me feel better than a whole box of Hardtack would." That was the discovery of the 128 volumes of *The War of The Rebellion: A Compilation of the Official Records of the Union and Confederate Armies* published in 1890, and the twelve-volume set of *The Rebellion Record: A Diary of American Events* published in 1865. Here was primary source material! What Henry's memoirs didn't tell me, I could learn firsthand from his commanding officers. I knew I had found my mission in life.

This is the story of Henry Brown Annis, a man of his time who was caught up in the times. An everyday dirt and grunt Union Army soldier, Henry, like many of his contemporaries, wrote of his experiences in the Civil War, waxing poetic with what the Civil War historian, Bruce Catton, describes as the "embroideries and purple passages of many an author of the time," and at the same time documenting the mundane, grub details of a soldier's existence. Throughout the memoirs, Henry's devotion to his country, his sense of humor, and his compassion shine through.

Henry enlisted in Company B, 96th Illinois Infantry on August 9, 1862. For nearly a year his regiment was relatively inactive, engaging in some minor skirmishes in Tennessee and, according to his army record, Henry spent three months in and out of hospitals in Ohio and Kentucky. Then, in the later part of the summer of 1863, the 96th Illinois and Henry were ordered to southeastern Tennessee, near Chattanooga, where the Union and Confederate forces were gathering for a showdown. The regimental history of the 96th Illinois and Henry Annis's military career revolved around this theater of action which, for the North, was an important turning point of the War. William Wood summed up the significance of the campaign when he wrote, "Chattanooga meant that the Union forces had at last laid the axe to the root of the tree."[*] The way was opened for Sherman's march to the sea.

Writing of his experience some years after the end of the War, Henry assumes, and rightfully so, that his readers had a grass roots familiarity with the "Battle Above the Clouds." To fully understand Henry Annis's experience, I have tried to put it into its larger context: The Chattanooga Campaign, which included the bloody, but indecisive "fracus," as Henry calls it, at Chickamauga, September 19 and 20, 1863; and its culmination on November 23, 24, and 25 in the Battle of Chattanooga where the fighting took place on Lookout Mountain and Missionary Ridge.

Using his memoirs and the official reports and correspondence documented in the volumes of *Official Records* and *The Rebellion Record*, I have attempted to

---

[*]*Captains of the Civil War* p. 281

retrace Henry's wartime experience and reconstruct it in the larger context of his regiment, and of the battles themselves. I have also tried to trace the personal and military history of the man who told it the way he fought it, learn about his superior officers who controlled not only the outcome of the battles, but Henry's fate as well, and clarify his experiences with both a micro and macro account of the battles and the interim siege, striving for an overall picture of this part of the Civil War and Henry Annis's part in it.

INTRODUCTION

The Battle of Chickamauga was a bloody disaster for both sides and a shaky victory for the South. By comparison, its aftermath, the Battle of Chattanooga, was one of the most picturesque battles of the War and a glorious victory for the North. Henry Annis fought in both, but years later when reflecting on his wartime adventures, he chose to write the account of his experience at Lookout Mountain which he briefly introduced and summarized in the first two pages of his memoirs.

There was a battle above the clouds November 24, 1863 on the sides of old Lookout Mountain as a large army can and will testify. The battle really commenced in the clouds, but was finished above its clouds.

The officers commanding the Federal forces were: General Hooker; General Geary, Division of 12th Army Corps; General Osterhaus, Division of 15th Army Corps; and General Whitaker's and General Grose's Brigades of the Fourth Army Corps, General Whitaker's Brigade having at that time ten regiments all engaged.

There certainly was a battle and somebody got hurt. Colonel W.F. Dowd of the 42nd Mississippi (Rebel) reported 199 killed and wounded from a total of 356. The 96th Illinois lost in killed and wounded 26, largely wounded. General Whitaker's Brigade captured two pieces of artillery near the Craven House and a large number of prisoners. So there must have been a battle, and we of the 96th Illinois, 8th Kentucky, and 40th Ohio of our Brigade were in the clouds at first. Else the sharpshooters on top of Lookout would have made sorry work for us a-shooting down from behind the rocks.

The whole side of the Mountain was enveloped almost in darkness with thick clouds in the early part of the day. Before two o'clock we had reached the eastern side of the mountain where we met the division of General Jackson (Confederate) who had come down off the Mountain to defend the Summerville Road and who gave us (Whitaker's men) a hard fight. Soon the clouds settled down and we saw the rocks above us. We were getting out of ammunition. Myself and some others were sent down on the side of the mountain towards Chattanooga to get some ammunition which had been brought on horseback as far as it could be. It was raining hard so that we got very wet and we could not see the Army that was below us.

As it very seldom rains without there being clouds, I think we may safely say there was a battle above the clouds on old Lookout. As for myself, I was there, and what's more stayed there on top of the Mountain for eight days and nights and nearly froze to death. The wind would blow our fires out as fast as we could build them. We had left our knapsacks and blankets near Wauhatchie before we attempted to climb the mountain.

The regiments that stayed on the Mountain to fortify and guard it were the 96th Illinois, and the 8th Kentucky whose flag was planted on the top of Lookout on the morning of the 25th, and showed to the army at Orchard Knob and Chattanooga boldly that they would not be shot in the back while charging on Mission Ridge.

I may truthfully say that it was not often the chance for a soldier in the ranks or out, to be out of danger and have such a splendid sight of so grand a movement of so many soldiers moving on almost impregnable works of a brave and determined effort, as when the Union Army moved on Mission Ridge on the 25th of November, 1863. The view that the 96th Illinois and the 8th Kentucky had from the top of the historic mountain may never and probably never will be repeated. May the Powers That Be grant that there will never be a necessity for it.

Table of Contents

Poem

We cannot appreciate that which is to come if we have no knowledge of what has gone before. History, our genetic memory, is our touchstone to the past, our understanding of the present, and our key to the future.

Chapter One
Henry Annis, Union Soldier

On August 9, 1862, Henry Brown Annis was a month to the day short of his thirty-first birthday when he volunteered to fight for his country. The Civil War was by then one year and four months old.

Born in Parishville, St. Lawrence County, in northern New York State to Nancy Tupper and Charles Annis on September 9, 1831, Henry had married Emma Sarah June at Brandon, Vermont in 1852 and taken up residence there, listing his occupation as that of farmer. The following year his eighteen year-old bride gave birth to Ella Lenett,[*] and two years later a boy, Willie Wesley[**] was born.

Sometime during the next two years the little family decided to pull up stakes and head West, for the record shows their next child, a girl named Carrie Francis, was born on Ella's fourth birthday, September 30, 1857 at Ringwood, Illinois. Then, on February 2nd, 1861, tragedy struck. Henry and Emma's only son, five and a half-year old Willie, died. But they had little time to dwell on that sorrow, for the following month their third girl, Marie Elizabeth,[***] was born at Volo Lake in Illinois. A year and a half later at Wauconda in Lake County, Illinois, Henry enlisted in Company B of the 96th Illinois Infantry for a term of three years.

---

[*] Ella was born September 3, 1853.
[**] Willie was born August 8, 1855.
[***] Marie Elizabeth was born March 10, 1861.

By the time Henry Annis was mustered into the army on September 5th at Rockford, the Civil War had been raging for seventeen months. Initial enthusiasm had waned, and hope for a speedy resolution of the conflict had vanished. The South, with its superior military skill, was beginning to give way to the more extensive strength of the North. Both armies had suffered crippling losses through casualties, desertions, and expirations of enlistments.

Chapter Two
This Is The Army

As the War dragged on, both the North and the South found it harder to recruit the disenchanted. Faced with the specter of conscription,* individual states, counties, and the Federal Government established bounties to attract volunteers. Despite its divided loyalties** the State of Illinois made an all-out effort to provide its quota of volunteers for the Cause of the Union. In addition to offering generous bounties,*** mass rallies were held in every village and town to encourage enlistments, and funds were raised to help the families of volunteers. Whatever their reasons for joining—to help the Union or to find adventure—the sons of Illinois responded, making conscription unnecessary in that state. A survey at the end of the War showed that the Land of Lincoln had provided

---

* On March 3, 1863, the Federal Government passed the Enrollment Act. This was the first instance of conscription or compulsory military service in the United States. A payment of $300.00 exempted a draftee. The Veteran Volunteer Act, passed early in 1864, provided that any man who re-enlisted would have free transportation home, a month's furlough, and a bounty of $400.00. On April 16, 1862, the Confederate Congress conscripted for three years' service all white males between 18 and 35 who were not legally exempt. The age was raised to 45 in September, and by February, 1864 the limits were 17 and 50.
** Many Southerners had moved into Southern Illinois (Cairo County) and were sympathetic to the Confederate Cause, threatening disunion.
*** Payment of bounties became a staggering tax burden for the state.

over one-quarter of a million men to fight and die (35,000 of them) for the Union.

The regiment was the building block of the army. Usually composed of men from the same area of the state, or of similar occupations, or from the same ethnic group, the regiments developed distinct personalities and an "esprit de regiment," a spirit unique to the Civil War. Henry Annis's regiment, the 96th Illinois, was raised mainly in Jo Daviess and Lake Counties in the northern part of the state. Colonel Thomas E. Champion of Warren, Illinois, was its commanding officer.

A regiment was generally made up of ten companies, alphabetically designated with the exception of "J." Henry belonged to Company B. The maximum authorized strength was 101 officers and men, the minimum, 83. They could recruit privates, but rather than replacing losses, new recruits were usually organized into new regiments. Company positions were generally obtained by election.* Henry was appointed sergeant of his regiment on August 23, 1862, and promoted to 4th sergeant on September 26th.

---

* They included a captain, first lieutenant, second lieutenant, one 1st sergeant, four sergeants, eight corporals, two musicians, and one wagoneer.

The authorized strength of infantry regiments was between 845 and 1,025 officers and men.[*] Regiments were organized into brigades which, in the Federal Army, averaged about 2,000 men. As most regiments were far below full strength, it took nearly five regiments to equal one brigade[**]. Two or more brigades were organized into a division averaging, in the Federal Army, 6,200 officers and men. Two or more divisions equaled a Corps.

In the Union an Army Corps included 45 infantry regiments and nine batteries of light artillery. The Corps were then assigned to one of the sixteen operational Union Armies which was named for the department or other territorial organization in which it operated.[***] Three of these armies were instrumental at Chattanooga. They were the Army of the Tennessee, the Army of the Potomac, and the Army of the Cumberland.

---

[*] The staff at regimental headquarters included a colonel (Col. Thomas E. Champion for the 96th Illinois), a lieutenant colonel, a major, an adjutant, a quartermaster, one surgeon, two assistant surgeons, and a chaplain. In addition, there were seven non-commissioned officers; a sergeant, major, quartermaster sergeant, commissary sergeant, hospital steward, and two principle musicians.

[**] Average regimental strength at Chickamauga on September 19-20, 1863 was 440.

[***] Confederate Corps were often named for their commanding officer. The Federals followed a general policy of naming their armies for the rivers near which they operated; the Confederates named theirs from the states or regions in which they were active. Thus, the Federals had an Army of <u>the</u> Tennessee—not to be confused with the Confederate Army of Tennessee. Both Tennessee Armies would face each other at Chattanooga.

Chapter Three
This is Tennessee

Until the summer of 1863, the Confederate Army had had the upper hand in the fighting, pushing as far north as Pennsylvania, then suffering at Gettysburg, the first of three major losses that year which would turn the tide of war for the North. On the same day in July that the Rebels were defeated at Gettysburg, Confederate General John C. Pemberton surrendered his army and the City of Vicksburg, Mississippi to General Grant. The third victory would be won at Chattanooga, Gateway to the Deep South.

The State of Tennessee played host to the second-most number of battles fought during the Civil War.[*] Like Illinois, Tennessee was in an uncomfortable political position as a border state. The eastern part of Tennessee was made up of small, cash-poor farmers who had little in common with the wealthy plantation owners, and were sympathetic to the Union Cause. Unlike Illinois, Tennessee was controlled by the Confederate forces which harassed these citizens, forcing many of them to hide in the mountains or flee to Kentucky. Lincoln had said to General Rosecrans, commander of the Army of the Cumberland, "If we can hold Chattanooga and East Tennessee, I think the Rebellion must dwindle and die."

Geographically, the topography of southeastern Tennessee presented some problems to both the conquering and defending armies. The Appalachian Ranges separates

---

[*] Virginia hosted the most.

the Atlantic portion of the southern states from the Mississippi Valley. Generally, these mountains or "folds in the earth's crust" run parallel to each other and at intervals are crossed by transverse depressions or gaps. Such passages or gateways are therefore of great commercial, political, and military importance. Like the "hawks nest" for which the Cherokee named it, the little town of Chattanooga was perched on one of these transverse depressions on the south bank of the Tennessee River, controlling the system of railroads that passed through it.

Outward from Chattanooga, the earth folds range in a southwesterly direction, their heights forming from west to east Sand or Raccoon Mountain, Lookout Mountain, Missionary Ridge, Pigeon Mountain, and Chickamauga Hills. The Chattanooga Valley is formed on the west by Lookout Mountain and on the east by Missionary Ridge.* The depression between Missionary Ridge and Pigeon Mountain forms the valley of Chickamauga.

---

* Years before, Catholic missionaries had build schools and churches on this ridge for the Cherokee, thus giving it its name.

Chapter Four
The Buildup in Tennessee

Since the beginning of the year, the Union Army of the Cumberland, commanded by Major General William S. Rosecrans, had been steadily pushing General Braxton Bragg's Confederate Army of Tennessee back from northern Tennessee, engaging it in battles at Murfreesboro[*] in January, and Tullahoma in June. Bragg was forced to evacuate Tullahoma on July 1 and withdraw toward Chattanooga where he established his headquarters. By August about 60,000 unproven Federals began to outflank the 47,000 tough, battle-wise Rebel troops at Chattanooga.[**]

Early in September, Rosecran's troops were split into three columns with flanks spread out more than forty miles apart over rough terrain and mountain ridges. Bragg missed his golden opportunity to dispatch the Union Army, one corps at a time, when his generals failed to carry out his orders. Rosecrans, realizing his danger, ordered a hurried concentration of the Army of the Cumberland that was completed by September 17. When the Union troops crossed the Tennessee River below Chattanooga, Bragg, not wishing to be cut off from his supplies and trapped in the city, moved his army to Lafayette, Georgia, about 20 miles south of Chattanooga to await reinforcements.

---

[*] Also known as Stone's River.
[**] See Appendix A.

During this time the 96th Illinois had experienced several reorganizations, but little action. On October 9, 1862, by special order from headquarters of the Department of the Ohio, the 96th Illinois was ordered to report to Cincinnati and from there proceed to Covington, Kentucky where they would report to Major-General Gordon Granger, Commanding, Army of Kentucky. The 96th Illinois "Return"[*] lists Henry Annis as "absent Sent to Marine Hospital, Cinn., Ohio Oct. 22."

By October 31st the troops of the Department of the Ohio had been organized with Major-General Horatio G. Wright, commanding. The 96th Illinois, under command of Colonel Thomas Champion, became a part of the Third Division, Army of Kentucky[**] which was commanded by Brigadier-General Absalom Baird. The Return for November shows Henry still sick in the hospital in Cincinnati.

In December of that year, General Baird reported the 96th as one of the regiments with him in Danville, Kentucky, "some regiments much reduced by sickness." The 96th Illinois was now part of the Second Brigade with Colonel J.C. Cochran in charge. The January 1863 Return reports Henry absent. "Left sick in Hosp. At Danville Ky. Jan. 26/63." It also shows that Henry was reduced to the

---

[*] "Return" was a part of the official army record of the Union soldier showing reason for absence on the Company Muster Roll. Other parts of the army record included "Company Descriptive Book," "Company Muster-in Roll," and "Company Muster-out Roll."
[**] Exception to Union army naming rule.

rank of a private soldier Feb. 10/63.[*] By March of 1863 the regiment had been sent to Tennessee where they experienced some minor skirmishes between March 4th and April 14th at Spring Hill, Triune, Liberty Gap, and Shelbyville.

As of June 8, 1863 "troops heretofore composing 4th Division, 14th Army Corps transferred to command of Maj. General Gordon Granger will be known as the Reserve Corps." As a result of this directive the 96th Illinois became part of the First Brigade, First Division. Among those regiments they were brigaded with were the 115th Illinois and the 40th Ohio with whom they would fight many battles.

On July 31st, 1863 the Reserve Corps was attached to the Department of Cumberland, General William Rosecrans commander. Baird was replaced by General Walter C. Whitaker as commander of the First Division. Colonel Champion was in charge of the First Brigade with Lieutenant Colonel Isaac L. Clark commanding the 96th Illinois. On August 25th, Henry was promoted to corporal and by August 31st the First Brigade, commanded temporarily by Colonel Champion in Whitaker's absence, along with the four regiments making up the Second Brigade, formed the First Division under the command of Brigadier-General James B. Steedman, a formidable man of great size and strength. Added to the First Division was McCook's Second Division. Together they equaled the Reserve Corps commanded by General Granger.

---

[*] Probably cause and effect.

Forty-one year-old Granger was considered to be outspoken, profane, rough in manner, and a rigid disciplinarian, but he possessed an insight and courage that would prove to be invaluable. Granger had led the Reserve Corps of the Cumberland at Tullahoma on June 8, 1863, and would gain his glory in leading them again at Chickamauga.

General Granger described the operations of his Reserve Corps leading up to the Battle of Chickamauga in the following report:

On the 6th instant, (September) I received orders from the general (Rosecrans) commanding the Army of the Cumberland to concentrate at Bridgeport, Alabama as much of my corps as could be spared from the duty of guarding the railroad, depots, and exposed points north of the Tennessee River...and from that point to move them to the support of the main body of the army. Two brigades of General Steedman's division were relieved from duty along the lines of railroad from Murfreesborough to Cowan, and from Wartrace to Shelbyville, by other troops from the rear.

On September third, the 96th Illinois was stationed at Estill Springs, Tennessee with the rest of their brigade strung out sixteen miles between Tullahoma and Cowan. Between September 7 and 17 they marched 32 miles to Stevenson, Alabama; then eight miles to Bridgeport, Alabama, arriving at Rossville, Georgia on the 17th where General Whitaker rejoined the brigade, resuming command, and General Granger headquartered, awaiting orders from General Rosecrans. In ten days the brigade had

11

marched 65 miles, "the whole distance," stated Granger, "through a suffocating dust and over a very rocky and mountainous road, on which it was exceedingly difficult for troops to travel." Positioned in Rossville, they were now five miles south of Chattanooga on Missionary Ridge. The Confederate Army was 18 miles south of them behind Pigeon Mountain at Lafayette, Georgia.[*]

Granger commented in his report:

The difficulties to be overcome in forwarding and in concentrating these troops, and in bringing forward others to partially supply their place in so short a period, can only be appreciated when the large space of country over which they were scattered, the great distance from which relief had to came, and the necessity of leaving no point of communication exposed, is fully known.

The Union troops were now within supporting distance of each other at Chickamauga, and the battle was brewing.

In eight months Rosecrans had succeeded in pushing Bragg back the length of Tennessee, nearly 90 miles, to his own front door, Chattanooga. Whoever controlled the city and its surrounding heights would control the railroads and river, and the destiny of the War. It was do or die. Bragg had to make a stand. Although he had withdrawn his army from Chattanooga, he had not retreated as Rosecrans was first led to believe. The Confederates were gradually gathering strength and waiting for their chance to force

---

[*] See Appendix A

Rosecrans southward, away from Chattanooga into a mountain cul-de-sac where his army could be destroyed.

Chapter Five
The "Fracus" at Chickamauga

Ten miles south of Chattanooga, across the border in Georgia, lies the Chickamauga Valley, a densely wooded area, thick with underbrush through which flows a creek of the same name. Chickamauga Creek rises at the junction of Missionary Ridge and Pigeon Mountain at the southern end of McLemore's Cove. Flowing northward down the Cove by Crawfish Spring and Lee and Gordon's Mill, this serpentine stream reaches the Lafayette and Chattanooga road where its sluggish current joins the main stream, emptying into the Tennessee River above Chattanooga. The Indian name, Chickamauga, means "River of Death."

On the night of September 18th, both armies were maneuvering for position. Strung out for a distance of four miles along the creek which flows roughly north and south, the Army of the Cumberland was positioned on the west side between Bragg's forces and Chattanooga. Their immediate objective was to guard the numerous crossings. Granger reported that at 4:00 that afternoon:

I ordered Brigadier-General Whitaker to move at once with his brigade and take possession of the crossing of the Chickamauga at Red House Bridge, and at the same time Col. Daniel McCook was ordered to march to the support of Col. Minty who was disputing the crossing of the Chickamauga at Reed's Bridge with the enemy. Col. McCook arrived within one mile of the bridge at dark, where he encountered the enemy, and with whom he had a slight skirmish, taking 22 prisoners.

According to Granger's report, Whitaker's mission wasn't as successful as McCook's.

General Whitaker was prevented from reaching the Red House Bridge by coming in contact with a superior force of the enemy on the road leading thereto. He had a severe skirmish, losing 60 men killed and wounded, but he held his ground until the next morning, when he received re-enforcements. The enemy, however, withdrew from his immediate front before daylight.

At daylight on the morning of the 19th Colonel McCook sent Lieutenant-Colonel Brigham, with the 69th Ohio Infantry, to surprise the enemy and gain possession of Reed's Bridge. Granger wrote of his action, "He gallantly charged across the bridge, drove the enemy from it, and destroyed it by fire."

As the enemy was gathering in force around Colonel McCook at Reed's Bridge, Granger sent him an order at 6:00 on the morning of the 19th to withdraw from that position. He then posted McCook's brigade at the junction of the Cleveland and Ringgold roads, covering the approaches to the rear and left flank of that part of his forces which were then on the road leading to the Red House Bridge. At the same time General Steedman was leading Mitchell's brigade to the assistance of General Whitaker. Granger concluded this part of his report on an ominous note:

Nothing further than slight skirmishing occurred in our front during the remaining part of the day. Yet, all indications led us to believe that a large force of the enemy confronted us.

Despite the efforts of Whitaker, McCook, and their counterparts along the creek to prevent the Rebels from crossing the Chickamauga, three-fourths of Bragg's men were over it by morning of the 19th.[*] The fighting began in earnest near Reed's Bridge when an infantry and cavalry accidentally ran into each other. The fighting was fierce, but poorly planned, the nature of the densely wooded battlefield making tactical control of the units all but impossible. Bragg, still awaiting his reinforcements, had all his units engaged in the battle. Rosecrans had provided for a reserve corps. Granger's two divisions were stationed at McAffee Church near Rossville waiting for orders to come to the aid of the Army of the Cumberland, if necessary.

Little progress was made the first day. Rosecrans manipulated his troops brilliantly, continually shifting them to his advantage, but by nightfall the issue was far from decided. There was much Union movement during the night as Rosecrans hurried to fill in his lines.

---

[*] By the next day there would be over 66,000 Confederate troops engaged in fighting the inferior Union force of 58,000. The odds were 5 to 4.

Chapter Six
Second Day of Battle

The second day of the battle, Sunday, September 20, started out badly for the Confederates. Bragg had planned to resume the battle at daybreak with an attack upon the Union lines, but again his subordinates failed to obey his orders and the fighting did not get underway until about 9:30.

As with the day before, both sides seemed destined to fight the indecisive battle forever, but then there occurred an exceedingly fortunate stroke of good luck coupled with the kind of irreparable blunder that turns generals' hair gray as well as turning the tide of battle. One division of Bragg's reinforcements, Longstreet's seasoned troops, finally arrived by rail. Detraining at Ringgold, they immediately set out towards the sound of battle. Meanwhile at Chickamauga, Rosecrans, the commander who had maneuvered his troops so masterfully the day before, lost track of where they were. An officer reported to him that Brannan's division was not in line, when they were, in reality, hidden in a more defensible position in the nearby wood. Without verifying this erroneous report, Rosecrans moved another regiment in position to cover the "gap," thus creating a real hole in the line and disaster for the Union forces.

As luck would have it, Longstreet's troops had just reached the field of battle and stumbled upon the hole in the Union line. Surging through it, they crushed the Federal flanks on either side. Thinking he was defeated, Rosecrans,

17

with his Generals Crittendon and Alexander McCook[*] fled the field with one-third of their troops, leaving Major-General George Thomas stranded and in command of the Union forces left behind.

General "Pap" Thomas, the man of many nicknames,[**] was about to earn himself another. Retreat for him was impossible. He had to stay and fight with what troops he could gather from the broken and scattered remnants of the Union Army. With characteristic determination, the six-foot tall, 200 pound former West Pointer organized a new line that was able to meet the fierce onslaught of Longstreet's troops, thus earning Thomas a new name, "The Rock of Chickamauga."[***]

Back at McAfee Church, Generals Granger and Whitaker listened to the unmistakable sounds of battle and waited in vain for orders to join it. Whitaker relates:

About 9:00 firing was heard in the direction of Crawfish Spring, on the Chickamauga. About 10:00 the firing of cannon and musketry took such direction as to

---

[*] Maj. Gen. Alexander McCook commanded the 12th Army Corps—not to be confused with Col. Daniel McCook, commander of the 2nd Division Reserve Corps.
[**] According to a contemporary, "Thomas was studious in his habits, deliberate, but decided in action and fastidious to the point of exasperation." His eccentricities afforded him many nicknames. While a cadet at West Point, he was known as "Old Tom" which was changed to "Slow Trot" when he became an instructor there.
[***] See Appendix B.

force us to the conclusion that our forces were being driven.

Granger waited for orders to attack, but none came. Instinctively, he reacted:

At 10:30 A.M. I heard heavy firing which was momentarily increasing in volume and intensity on our right, in the direction of General Thomas's position. Soon afterward, being well convinced, judging from the sound of battle, that the enemy were pushing him hard, and fearing that he would not be able to resist their combined attack, I determined to go to his assistance at once. It was now about 11:00 A.M. I started with Gen. Whitaker's and Col. Mitchell's brigades, under the immediate command of Gen. Steedman, and left Col. McCook's brigade at the McAfee Church in position to cover the Ringgold road.

Whitaker, his brigade in the lead, continued the account:

With alacrity and enthusiasm the men marched under a hot sun and through clouds of dust up the Lafayette road until they found the Rebel mounted infantry drawn up in line of battle to intercept our progress. They had already reached the rear of Gen. Thomas's command and had possession of the field hospital, which they had most inhumanly shelled while filled with our wounded, killing my personal friend, the gallant Dick Rockingham (lieutenant-colonel of my brave old regiment, the 6th Kentucky Infantry) who was lying in it, wounded. Arriving between twelve and one P.M. at the point occupied by General

Thomas, we found him sorely pressed and yielding stubbornly to superior numbers.

Steadman's two brigades reached the end of the Union right flank just as the Confederate commanders were massing their troops for another assault. Granger describes Thomas's precarious situation:

His forces were at that time stationed upon the brow of and holding a horseshoe ridge. * *The enemy were pressing him hard in front and endeavoring to turn both of his flanks. General Thomas had not the troops to oppose this movement of the enemy, and in fifteen minutes from the time when we appeared on the field, had it not been for our fortunate arrival, his forces would have been terribly cut up and captured. As rapidly as possible I formed General Whitaker's and Col. Mitchell's brigades, to hurl them against this threatening force of the enemy which afterward proved to be General Hindman's division.*

Whitaker formed his command in two lines, the 96th Illinois on the right, the 115th Illinois in the center, the 22nd Michigan on the left of the first line; the 40th Ohio on the right, the 84th Indiana in the center, and the 89th Ohio on the left of the second line.

Both lines advanced at a double-quick pace against the enemy. The conflict was terrific. The enemy was driven near half a mile. Rallying, they drove my command a short distance when they, in turn, were driven again with great loss. Both lines had been thrown into the conflict on the

---

* Also known as Snodgrass Hill

second charge, and the whole line kept up a deadly and well-directed fire upon the enemy who fought with great determination and vigor.

Granger vividly described the drama exploding around him:

The gallant Steedman, seizing the colors of a regiment, led his men to the attack. With loud cheers they rushed upon the enemy and, after a terrific conflict lasting but twenty minutes, drove them from their ground and occupied the ridge and gorge. The slaughter of both friend and foe was frightful. * *General Whitaker, while rushing forward at the head of his brigade, was knocked from his horse by a musket-ball and was for a short time rendered unfit for duty, while two of his staff officers were killed, and two mortally wounded.*

General Steedman's horse was killed, and he was severely bruised, yet he was able to remain on duty during the day. This attack was made by our troops, very few of who had ever been in an action before, against a division of old soldiers who largely outnumbered them. Yet with resolution and energy they drove the enemy from his strong position, occupied it themselves, and afterward held the ground they had gained with such terrible losses. The victory was dearly won, but to this army it was a priceless one.

After a short lull in the battle, Granger's Reserves were attacked by two divisions of Longstreet's veterans. Again,

---

* In the first 30 minutes, the 96th lost 100 men, including six out of nine officers and eight of their nine color bearers.

the enemy was driven back, and from this time until dark the battle between these two opposing forces raged furiously.

Our whole line was continually enveloped in smoke and fire. The assaults of the enemy were now made with that energy which was inspired by the bright prospect of a speedy victory and by a consciousness that it was only necessary to carry this position and crush our forces to enable him to overthrow our army and drive it across the Tennessee River. Their forces were massed and hurled upon us for the purpose of terminating at once this great and bloody battle. But the stout hearts of the handful of men who stood before them as a wall of fire, quailed not. They understood our perilous position and held their ground, determined to perish rather than yield it. Never had a commander such just cause for congratulation over the action of his troops.

Running low on ammunition, Granger's Reserve troops were forced to scavenge the cartridge boxes of their own and the enemy's dead and wounded. This supply was soon exhausted and still the enemy was at their front, hurling fresh troops against them. Granger continues his account:

It was almost dark; the enemy had been driven back, but we had not a round of ammunition left. All now seemed to be lost if he should return to the contest. Anticipating another attack. I ordered the command to be given to the men to stand firm and to use the cold steel. After an ominous silence of a few minutes the enemy came rushing upon us again. With fixed bayonets our troops gallantly charged them and drove them back in confusion. Twice more were these charges repeated and the enemy driven back before darkness brought an end to the battle. Night came and the enemy fell back, whipped and discomfited.

Thanks to the timely intervention of Granger's Reserve Corps, the remainder of the Army of the Cumberland, rallied by Thomas, the "Rock of Chickamauga," was able to retreat in an orderly way and live to fight another day.

Chapter Seven
After Chickamauga

The outcome of Chickamauga was a questionable Confederate victory, but Bragg refused to follow up his advantage. Longstreet had asked Bragg for reinforcements while fighting Thomas's and Granger's men at Horseshoe Ridge. Bragg refused. Generals Polk and Longstreet urged immediate pursuit of the retreating Union Army. Bragg refused. Again the next day, General Forrest, observing the chaos and disorder of the Union Army, urged the stubborn Bragg to take pursuit. Still he refused, relieving Forrest of his command and recommending court-martial.

Bragg's unfortunate personality and questionable leadership abilities inspired little confidence or cooperation from his officers and much hatred from the men under his command. He operated with little knowledge of the enemy and seldom checked on progress of the battle or execution of his orders, which were often ignored, diminishing his effectiveness. He regularly blamed subordinates for his failures, often relieving senior officers at whim. In addition to recommending court-martial for Forrest, Bragg relieved Polk, D.H. Hill, and Hindman for unsatisfactory performances during the campaign.

The Battle of Chickamauga was one of the bloodiest battles of the Civil War. Out of a total of 125,000 participants there were over 34,000 casualties; 18,000 Confederate and 16,000 Union soldiers killed, wounded, or missing, both sides chalking up almost the same 28% casualty figures. Although the Confederates technically "won," Lieutenant General D.H. Hill, Confederate Corps commander, saw Chickamauga for what it was—"a worthless victory." The fight at the "River of Death" was a defeat for both sides. The dispute over Chattanooga was still to be resolved.

Wars are costly. The official comment in the Itinerary for Whitaker's First Brigade notes, "September 20 (Sunday): Fought the Battle Chickamauga with honor and credit to itself. The losses of the command in the engagement were 1,170 in killed, wounded, and missing." In line of battle only three hours, the ten regiments and two batteries of Steedman's Division lost about half their force. It cost nearly 500 men an hour to save the Army of the Cumberland.

Whitaker's command had "...the honor of bringing from that gory field the flags of our brave corps commander (Granger) and of our gallant division commander (Steedman), all proudly floating by that (flag) of the First Brigade." Whitaker continues:

Our loss was heavy. It could not be otherwise. We fought, as I have been informed by prisoners, three divisions of the enemy, two of which were from Longstreet's corps. They fought like tigers, and with a zeal and energy worthy of a better cause...The enemy's loss far exceeded ours.

Before Chickamauga, Whitaker's Brigade numbered 2,877 rank and file. At Chickamauga he lost in killed, missing, or wounded, 1,270 or 44% of his effective force. All of his staff officers but one were killed or wounded in battle. The 96th Illinois with 402 in battle, lost 225, including Lt. Col. Isaac L. Clarke who was killed, suffering a 56.1% casualty figure.[*] Whitaker concluded in his official report of the battle:

The honored dead I mourn. To the living I tender my warmest thanks on behalf of our country for their courage and faithfulness in the face of the foe. I hope it will not be considered beyond the scope of a report to congratulate the great States of Illinois, Ohio, Michigan, and Indiana upon the courage, efficiency, and fidelity with which their sons, composing my command, have sustained the honor of their respective States and served our common country.

Chickamauga was a maker and breaker of reputations. Thomas, a Virginian who had been Bragg's lieutenant in the Mexican War, finally earned the trust of his fellow Union officers, and proved both his loyalty to the Union and his courage in battle. In his commendation Rosecrans named him "the true soldier, the prudent and undaunted commander, the modest and incorruptible patriot. To him the thanks and gratitude of the country are due for his conduct at the Battle of Chickamauga."

Ironically, within a month Rosecrans would be relieved of his command and replaced by Thomas.

Although history credits Thomas with saving the Army of the Cumberland, it was Granger's Reserve Corps that saved Thomas. Of Granger, Rosecrans said, "He, by his promptitude, arrived and carried his troops into action in

---

[*] Henry Annis was also among the wounded.

time to save the day. He deserves the highest praise." For his remarkable performance at Chickamauga, Granger was elevated to command of a corps.

General Thomas spoke of General James Steedman as the one who "valiantly maintained Brannan's right," and Granger calls attention "to the bravery and gallantry displayed during the battle by him," and says, "He fearlessly rushed into the midst of danger and was ever present with his troops, handling them with ease, rallying them, and encouraging them, and established order and confidence."

General Granger commended General Whitaker as "conspicuous for his bravery and activity, managing his troops well, and contributing much to our success." General Thomas recommended him for promotion for "the gallant and obstinate defense made…in the Battle of Chickamauga against overwhelming numbers of the enemy."

Colonel Champion who stated in his report of the battle, "If I had had 500 men, I could have driven the enemy completely from the field," was commended by General Granger as "most conspicuous for efficiency and deserving special mention."

Rosecrans did not receive any such accolades. The defeat at Chickamauga cost him his command. Three of his generals, McCook, Crittenden, and Negley, who prematurely fled the field at Chickamauga with him, were also relieved of command and charged with misconduct. They were later acquitted.

Chapter Eight
Union Army Under Siege at Chattanooga

After the disaster at Chickamauga, the Union Army withdrew to Chattanooga, digging in to establish a fortress. Bragg had previously fled the city to avoid entrapment. Now Rosecrans found himself effectively walled in by the Tennessee River on the north, Raccoon and Lookout Mountains to the south and southwest, the long, attenuated slope called Missionary Ridge to the east, and to the south the bloody field from which they had just fled, Chickamauga.

One hundred miles to the north of the Army of the Cumberland was another Union army under the command of General A.E. Burnside. It was stationed in Knoxville by order of President Lincoln to protect the loyal people of Eastern Tennessee. Without firing a gun, this army would prove to be an important factor in defeating the Rebels at Lookout Mountain and Missionary Ridge.

Bragg established his Confederates in the heights surrounding Chattanooga, and thus gained control of the roads and railroads leading into the city, cutting the Union supply lines in an attempt to starve them out. The Union Army was under siege in Chattanooga, the city it had tried to wrest from the Confederacy.

Of strategic importance, the Tennessee River, named for the village of Cherokee originally located on it, flows southwest from its origin in Knoxville. Passing north of Chattanooga, it flows southward along the west side of the city for about two miles before reaching Lookout Mountain. There, it curves northward forming an elongated loop known as Moccasin Point. The river continues its northward course to Brown's Ferry, and then divides to flow around Williams's Island. Rejoining itself, the waterway curves westward around the northern end of Raccoon Mountain and resumes its southwest meandering past Kelly's Ferry, through Bridgeport, Alabama, and into the strategically important Western Confederacy.[*]

Kelly's Ferry and Brown's Ferry are located seventeen river miles from each other. Overland, through a pass in Raccoon Mountain, the distance is seven miles. Establishing this overland route would mean the difference between success or starvation for the Union Army. Unfortunately, it would be a lean and hungry month for Rosecran's command before this could be accomplished.

Meanwhile, both sides were digging in and fortifying their positions. The itinerary of Whitaker's First Brigade stated that on September 22nd (Tuesday), "The command was ordered to occupy the hill opposite Chattanooga... The 96th Illinois Volunteers was sent to guard the ferry and crossing on the river at William's Ferry." They received further instructions to "guard and organize the trains on the north side of the river...taking especial pains to stop all stragglers and organize them, permitting none to pass beyond their lines without satisfactory authority."

The next day the "Rebels fired on the...ferry boat. The hands jumped overboard leaving her so that she drifted to

---

[*] See Appendix B.

shore and fell into their possession." The game of "take-away" continued. On September 24th Whitaker reported:

A body of Rebels, clothed in Federal uniforms, approached the river this morning at the crossing near the base of Lookout Mountain and succeeded in capturing the boat which was being moved to a better position by a squad of 34 men. But the regiment, which I had stationed on this side at that point, opened fire upon the Rebels and made it so hot as to compel them to leave the boat which I now have in my possession.

While Whitaker's men were busy with the boat and guarding the crossing, (the command was now distributed along the river between Brown's and William's Ferries) the enemy was busy annoying them, first with sharpshooters concealed among the rock and brush on the slope of the mountain, firing haphazardly at his officers and men. Then they became a real threat after setting up a "battery of heavy 24-pounded rifled guns in the earth work on the east slope of Lookout Mountain, completely commanding all the positions of our artillery. Their fire is very accurate..." The 96th had their hands full protecting the ferry, dodging shot and shell, and trying to get the tools to casemate their guns and make their position secure.

At the beginning of the siege, the Union army had an ample supply of goods on hand. Transporting them over the road from Bridgeport to Chattanooga seemed quite feasible at first.[*] Then, in early October came a natural disaster in the form of rains making the roads nearly impassable. A Confederate by the name of Wheeler proved to be an even worse disaster. Hundreds of Union wagons and animals attempting to bring in supplies were harassed and destroyed by him. Times became tough. Transport animals—mules and horses—died by the score for lack of forage and troops subsisted on moldy corn and whatever they could scavenge. There were so many dead animals lying where they had dropped that the Union soldiers maintained the best way to travel the muddy, rain-swollen roads was to jump from muleback to muleback.[**]

---

[*] Chattanooga, Tennessee; Bridgeport, Alabama; and Chickamauga, Georgia form a triangle where the three states come together. The Chattanooga-Bridgeport leg of the triangle equals about 25 miles, the Bridgeport-Chickamauga leg about the same, and the Chickamauga-Chattanooga leg, ten miles.

[**] An article appearing in the Chattanooga Gazette offered an interesting conjecture concerning discovery of the remains of the dead animals many geologic years hence: "ANOTHER SNAKE STORY—Between the Point of Lookout Mountain and Bridgeport, down the Valley of the Tennessee, lie twenty-five miles of dead mules in one continuous string, the head of the first carcass lying on the 'quarter-deck' of the one beyond him, and so on throughout the entire distance. Just imagine a convulsion of nature of sufficient magnitude to bury these remains as they now lie, and phancy the pheelings of a future Agassiz, who, in his geological researches, strikes either of the termini, and attempts to exhume the entire 'snake.' Won't it knock the socks off the saurians of the Diluvium Period? Twenty-five miles of vertebrae with two pedal arrangements every three feet! What a bully side show for a future circus! It will probably be called 'the old he-Copperhead of the Rebellion period' admission ten cents—Peace Democrats half price."

Henry Annis described this situation and these conditions as he began the account of his "Experience At and On Lookout Mountain."

The Battle of Lookout Mountain was not our first acquaintance with the Historic Pile with its Peak among the clouds. On the 16ᵗʰ of September, 1863, we, the 96ᵗʰ Illinois, with the balance of General Gordon Granger's Reserve Corps and other troops climbed its rugged side and over its shoulder down into the valley on our way to join in the little fracus which came off at Chickamauga on the 18ᵗʰ, 19ᵗʰ, and 20ᵗʰ of September, 1863.

After we had made hash of the Jony Rebs over there and being badly hashed up ourselves, we came back by way of Rossville and along the base of Mission Ridge through Chattanooga, crossed the Tennessee River, and took up our quarters on the Historical Moccasin Point, it being just across the Tennessee River from Lookout Mountain. And all together too close for our comfort or convenience, the fellows who lived over there were bound to get acquainted or pick a fight with us. for no sooner did we show camp or try to make coffee and stew our swine belly, than they began to throw shell and shot from the top of Lookout Mountain where they had several batteries so placed as to allow them to drop shell directly into our camp, if it could be called a camp. For we had left our tents, blankets and overcoats, and not a few of our comrades, over at the place called Chickamauga.

They even said they would starve us out and they came so near it that it makes me hungry now to think of it. But we were not idle. We built a little fort or a protection for a battery and hauled by hand the 18th Ohio battery up onto or into the rocks on Moccasin Ridge. This battery put in their work well, but the Rebs made it a little warm for them. So the 9th Ohio and 10th Indiana batteries were placed there and all were made bombproof by the infantry. With these three batteries well manned, it made the Rebs a little cautious, for so good was our aim that we cut down their signal flag and dismounted one of their guns.

In the meantime our enemies were a-getting in their work well toward the starvation business. We stood that kind of racket for thirty days. Our diet had been principally corn, and very poor corn at that, too soft and mouldy to shell. Our neighbors offered and even tried to shell it for us, but we chose to roast it and gnaw it from the cob.

Chapter Nine
Help Is On The Way

The War Department in Washington D.C. considered the siege of the Union Army at Chattanooga critical. A high-level emergency meeting called the night of September 23rd, rousted President Lincoln from his bed. Lincoln, Secretary of War Stanton, and members of the Cabinet resolved to detach the 11th and 12th Army Corp from the Army of the Potomac. Under the command of General Hooker, this force was to go to the aid of the Army of the Cumberland that was trapped in Chattanooga. Traveling 1,157 miles by rail with 20,000 troops and more than 3,000 horses and mules, Hooker's detachment arrived in Bridgeport, Alabama between September 30th and the middle of October.

At the same time General Sherman, stationed at Vicksburg, Mississippi, received orders to report to Bridgeport with his three divisions of 17,000 men composing the 15th Army Corps of the Army of the Tennessee.[*] He embarked on October 3rd by boat, traveling 200 miles north on the Mississippi to Memphis. From Memphis he traveled east by railroad alternating the 475 miles between northern Mississippi and Alabama and northern Tennessee arriving in Bridgeport November 15th. The combined troop movements of Hooker and Sherman to reinforce besieged Rosecrans were a triumph of skill and

---

[*] Army of the Tennessee was Grant's former command.

planning.[*] Two experienced armies stood at the ready to help the still-green Army of the Cumberland.

Major-General Ulysses S. Grant was put in charge of the newly created Military Division of the Mississippi, arriving in Chattanooga October 23rd to take personal charge of the situation there. The Army of the Cumberland was reorganized with Thomas succeeding Rosecrans as the commanding general. The Fourth Army Corps, a consolidation of McCook and Crittenden's men, was now commanded by General Gordon Granger. Brigadier-General Charles Cruft commanded the First Division. This time Whitaker had charge of the 2nd Brigade which included the 96th Illinois, again commanded by Colonel Thomas E. Champion who, along with Major George Hicks, commanded the 35th Indiana, 8th Kentucky, 40th Ohio, 51st Ohio, and 99th Ohio. The 3rd Brigade was commanded by Colonel William Grose.

When Rosecrans was in command, the Army of the Cumberland had been powerless to lift the siege and bring in the badly needed supplies to Chattanooga. With the arrival of Grant, along with Hooker's and Sherman's armies, plans were shaped and effected to lift the siege and reestablish a supply route to Chattanooga.

During the night of October 26-27, 1,500 troops floated down-river from Chattanooga on pontoon boats, sneaking past Confederate positions and landing at Brown's Ferry, three miles below Lookout Mountain. At the same time another force was marching across Moccasin Point to

[*] See Appendix C

support the river-borne troops. Upon disembarking at Brown's Ferry, the pontoon troops drove off the Confederate sharpshooters on the west bank, threw up a breastworks, and with the help of the earth-bound troops, constructed a pontoon bridge across the river. Coinciding with this action, Hooker advanced from Bridgeport driving the Confederate forces back from Raccoon Mountain, and Brigadier-General John W. Geary remained at Wauhatchie to guard the road to Kelly's Ferry.

Now the way was clear to open a short supply line between Bridgeport and Chattanooga. In *Chickamauga and Chattanooga Battlefields* Sullivan described the route of this supply line, or "Cracker Line" as it was dubbed by the hungry troops. "This Cracker Line ran by boat up the Tennessee River from Bridgeport to Kelley's Ferry. Above Kelley's Ferry the swift current made the stream unnavigable at certain points. Accordingly, at Kelley's Ferry, the Cracker Line left the river and crossed Raccoon Mountain by road to Brown's Ferry. There it crossed the river on the pontoon bridge, thence across Moccasin Point, and finally across the river once more into Chattanooga." In *The Civil War Dictionary,* Boatner describes its effect: "The morning of 30 Oct. the steamboat Chattanooga arrived at Kelley's Ford with 40,000 rations and tons of forage. The cry went up from the troops: 'The Cracker line open. Full rations, boys!'"

Henry Annis well remembered the reorganization of the troops and the opening of the Cracker Line.

On the 23 of October General Grant came to Chattanooga, and on the 27th a fleet of boats came down the river and before daylight was anchored near Brown's Ferry and was there made into a bridge on which we crossed to assist fighting for Hooker who was coming up from the west to Lookout Valley on the 28th and 29th. There was some very sharp fighting which resulted in opening up our Cracker Line to Bridgeport. On the thirtieth we recrossed the river to our old camp with our haversacks full of good sound corn that we got at Wauhatchie. The next day we started for Shellmound where we got full rations.

Previous to this there had been a reorganization of the troops in the field. General Whitaker's Brigade, to which the 96th Illinois was still attached, became the Second Brigade of the First Division of the Fourth Army Corps. The 11th Illinois, the 40th Ohio, and the 84th Indiana were of the old brigade. The 54th and 98th Ohio, 35th Indiana, and 8th Kentucky were now brigaded with us.

We arrived at Shellmound the next day and camped at the mouth of the Cave which is a natural curiosity, being 300 feet wide, 500 feet deep, and 75 feet high. Beyond this Grand Hall and turning sharp to the left, it becomes narrow and extends a long ways into the mountain out of which comes a very cold, clear stream of water. We camped beside this stream and prepared to cook the rations which had been promised us. General Whitaker gave orders to the Captain of Commissary located there to issue rations to the 2nd Brigade, 1st Division of the 4th Army Corps. The officer said that he did not know any such command. Well, Whitaker said that he did. Whitaker came back and ordered the Bloody 35th Indiana to fall in fix bayonets, and we got the rations and filled up full for once.

The 96th Illinois and the 40th Ohio then went three miles up to Nicojack Cove for camp and guard duty and built us a shanty city. We stayed there, occasionally going on a scouting tramp, until the 19th of November. On the 19th we drew six days rations and were ordered to be ready to march at a moment's notice. General Sherman's army was marching by, toward Chattanooga. Well, we marched out of camp and back again, got mad, and got over it again, until the 23rd when we packed up and commenced the tramp which took us to Wauhatchie, on Lookout Break, near the base of Lookout Mountain on which we could see the Rebel campfires burning. We had not been told what was expected of us, but being quite well-acquainted with the topography of Old Lookout and seeing the campfires on the mountaintop and sides, and the general movement of troops, in fact, the very atmosphere made us have a peculiar feeling up and down our spinal column. At this particular time we had but a single captain in our whole regiment, Captain Taylor of Company E, a result of the fracus over the Hill.

Chapter Ten
The Generals Prepare For a Rematch

Early in November, Bragg met with his superior and chief and probably only supporter, Confederate President Jefferson Davis. Upon viewing the half-starved troops and animals of the Army of the Cumberland, they concurred that they had the Union Forces well in hand. So on November 4th Bragg ordered General Longstreet with his 200,000 troops (1/3 of his army) to Knoxville to take care of Burnside.[*] Later in the month he weakened his force on Lookout Mountain by relieving those troops he suspected of having loyalties to Eastern Tennessee.

General Grant had known Braxton Bragg fifteen years before in the Mexican War. From that time on their careers had gone in quite opposite directions; Bragg had resigned from the army in 1856 and successfully run his plantation, at the same time designing a drainage and levee system for the State of Louisiana. Joining the militia in 1861, he was commissioned colonel and then promoted to major-general. In June of '62 he replaced Beauregard as Commander of Army of Tennessee, ineptly leading Bragg's invasion of Kentucky and continuing his downhill course in the battles at Perryville, Stones River, Tullahoma, and Chickamauga.

Ulysses Grant, on the other hand, showed little initial promise in either his military career or in his personal life.

---

[*] Possibly in retaliation for their clash at Chickamauga. Without firing a gun, this army proved to be an important factor in defeating the Rebels at Lookout Mountain and Missionary Ridge.

After finishing the Mexican War as a captain, he was stationed on the West Coast. Out of loneliness for his wife and children, he began drinking and neglecting his duty. Only his resignation in 1854 saved him from a court-martial.

His personal life fared no better as he failed at a number of undertakings and became destitute. Volunteering for the Union Army in 1861, Grant was eventually given command as colonel of the 21st Illinois. His ability to handle troops and supplies, coupled with his ability to take initiative, fight aggressively, and make quick decisions, destined Grant for greater things. His career was clearly on the rise. Conversely, Bragg's incompetence could no longer be denied. His career was rapidly deteriorating.

The Battle of Chickamauga, under the direction of Rosecrans and Bragg, started by mistake and was characterized by blunders. The Battle of Chattanooga was carefully orchestrated and brilliantly conducted by General Grant. The performance was scheduled to begin November 21st, but heavy rains delayed the attack until November 23rd. The preliminaries began at 2:00 P.M. that day when Sheridan's and Wood's divisions captured Orchard Knob, a low hill a little more than a mile in front of Missionary Ridge. Grant established his headquarters there the next day from whence he could conduct the battles.

Chapter Eleven
The Battle of Chattanooga
Acts 1 and 2: Lookout Mtn., Nov. 23, 24

Act One began on the night of November 23-24 with Sherman crossing his army at Brown's Ferry. From there Smith's Brigade marched overland to North Chickamauga Creek to man the pontoon boats previously concealed at its confluence with the Tennessee. Once across the river they secured a bridgehead at the mouth of the South Chickamauga Creek and built bridges over which the remainder of Sherman's army would march. By 4:00 P.M. the Army of the Tennessee had attacked and seized the north end of Missionary Ridge. As Grant's left wing, their objective was to seize Tunnel Hill, which they would accomplish with difficulty the next day.[*]

Act Two took place on Lookout Mountain on the 24th of November. The scene of this action, Lookout Mountain, rises 2,146 feet above sea level at the Moccasin Bend of the Tennessee River near Chattanooga, and drops precipitously several hundred feet from a plateau 1,100 feet above the river. The top of the mountain was held by two Confederate brigades of Cheatham's Division, one blocking the narrow passage around the northern face of the mountaintop, the other occupying the adjacent slope.

The taking of Lookout Mountain, except for the crest, was surprisingly simple, but ranks as one of the most thrilling moments of the War. The original plans were to

---

[*] See Appendix D.

merely hold Lookout Valley. This was changed when high
water broke the pontoon bridge at Brown's Ferry during
Sherman's crossing, leaving one of his divisions,
Osterhaus's, high and dry. Unable to fight with Sherman,
this division was assigned to Hooker, and orders were
given to take Lookout Mountain and descend into
Chattanooga Valley.

The Union forces chosen to storm the mountain were
made up of divisions from all three armies. The First
Division of the Fourth Army Corps, commanded by
Brigadier-General Charles Cruft, represented the Army of
the Cumberland. The Army of the Potomac was
represented by the Second Division of the 12th Army
Corps, commanded by Brigadier-General John W. Geary.
Peter J. Osterhaus commanded the First Division, 15th
Corps of the Army of the Tennessee, the division that had
not been included in the original plans. These three
divisions, all strangers to each other, were commanded by
Major-General "Fighting Joe Hooker." They constituted
Grant's right wing.

The 96th Illinois was a part of the two brigades
representing the Army of the Cumberland in the assault
upon Lookout Mountain. Their brigade, with 1,465 actively
engaged, was commanded by General Whitaker, the other
commanded by Colonel William Grose.

According to General Whitaker, the preparations for the
day of battle began at 9:00 A.M. on November 23rd when
the six regiments under his command left Shellmound.
Marching 23 miles over rough roads, they reported to
General Cruft, division commander, at the base of Raccoon

Mountain near the mouth of Lookout Creek. For reasons unknown to Whitaker, the two brigades of General Cruft's division were divided, and his, the Second Brigade, reported to General Geary on the morning of the 24th. After first massing under cover of the hills near Wauhatchie, the troops crossed Lookout Creek on the dam of a little mill. They were ordered to leave their knapsacks and blankets under guard in preparation for the anticipated battle.

Whitaker describes the line of battle as follows: "2nd brigade of General Geary's division in front on the right, 3rd brigade in the center, and the first brigade on the extreme left and near the base of the mountain." Of Whitaker's brigade the 8th Kentucky formed the extreme right at the base of rough projecting crags, the 35th Indiana next, then the 99th Ohio and the 40th Ohio on his extreme left. The 96th Illinois and 51st Ohio were placed next to General Geary's right, 600 yards to the rear of Whitaker's right. The lines of the entire storming party were placed in echelon,* with the front protected by skirmishers. The danger in this arrangement was that Whitaker's brigade "occupying the position nearest the apex of the cone had a shorter route in going around the mountain than those nearest its base." This could enable them to overtake and pass the front line.

The climb up the mountain was the greatest problem for the advancing regiments. Whitaker describes the rigorous three-mile advance of his brigade over the steep, rocky ravines and torrent-torn sides of the mountain:

---

* A step-like arrangement

It was laborious and extremely tiresome. The enemy was found sheltered by rocks, trees, and timber cut to form abattis or obstructions, while the summit of the mountain was covered with sharpshooters concealed by the overhanging cliffs. Attacking with vigor, we drove them before us. One of the enemy's camps being assailed by General Geary's command lower down the mountain, numbers of them fled toward the summit of the mountain and were captured by this brigade. They did not conceive it possible for a force to advance on the ground my brigade was then covering.

Steadily, but energetically and firmly advancing, my brigade reached the crest of Lookout's bold projecting slope. Its profile is delineated from beneath against the sky. In good order my bold command now became one line, swung round the crest, the right being the pivot, with the flags of the 40ᵗʰ Ohio on the left, and of the 8ᵗʰ Kentucky on the right floating free and triumphant.

Whitaker's brigade was ordered forward to the crest of Lookout to assail the rifle pits there. The Confederates resisted so stubbornly that hand-to-hand combat ensued in portions of the entrenchment. Finally, Whitaker's regiments were able to drive the Rebels along the side and down the mountain, between a quarter and half mile beyond the White House, [*] over breastworks, ravines, and rocks. Lookout Mountain was theirs!

---

[*] Also referred to as the Craven House, Whitaker estimated it to be a kind of palatial resort for Rebels.

The day was a memorable one for Henry Annis. He documents it in his memoirs:

The morning of the 24th came and with it a fog so dense that we could not see the mountain or anything but a few rods away. At our early hour we were in line, our Colonel Champion from the back of his horse made a speech, a short one. He said, "Boys, before night I expect we will have to climb the sides of yonder mountain. Remember Chickamauga. I expect every man to do his whole duty. I shall try to do mine."

All eyes were lifted toward Lookout, and the rugged giant seemed to answer the Colonel's speech. Standing on his Beam of Rock with his cloudy toga wrapped around him, he seemed to say to the five states and two armies at his feet that Human Valor could not prevail against his natural strength.

But the time for action had come and we set to work to gaining a secret side entrance to that lofty stage or Theatre of War. General Hooker's command started in near the Tennessee River with General Geary's Division of the 15th Army Corps, and Whitaker's and Grose's brigades of the 4th Army Corps with

General Charles Cruft as division commander and General Gordon Granger, corps commander.

The general plan was that General Hooker should make a direct front attack on the face of the Rebel works with General Wood[*] on his (Hooker's) left flank, and that a flanking force should go to the right. It fell to our lot, Whitaker's brigade, with the 96th Illinois on the right and Geary's division on the left of the flanking force.

From Wauhatchie we marched up Lookout Valley under cover of the fog, unslung and piled up our knapsacks and all extra weight we could spare. We then crossed Lookout Creek and made our way as best we could through the deep rocky ravines, brush and thorns. After a hard pull we, with torn hands and bleeding and bruised skins, reached the Palisades. We then came to a battlefront with our right resting near the perpendicular rocks which rose grimly above us, our lines stretching far down the slope toward the creek. We then advanced towards the Rebel works, sweeping the entire side of the

---

[*] General Wood was a commander of one of Osterhaus's brigades.

mountain. It seemed to me the roughest ground I had ever marched over, and I think my regiment had the roughest ground of any, being on the right and nearest the enemy with the crack of the sharpshooters' rifle and the whiz of the ball as they sent them from the cliff 100 feet above us down the line.

The attention of the Rebel army in the works was diverted from us by Osterhaus who was engaged in forcing a crossing directly in his front, or from the top of the mountain above us. But soon heavy skirmishing began on our left toward the base of the mountain. Grose was forcing his way across the creek. General Wood was rousing his battlefront for a climb into the clouds above the Rebel works. At eleven O'clock our left had connected with Osterhaus's right and the alignment of battle was complete from the Palisades to the mountain base. Thence curving away towards the northern end of Lookout, a Sickle of Mars whose Blue Blade and fire-tipped edge was that day to sweep around its point as a pivot and reap a glorious harvest.

The Battle Above the Clouds was fought on a plateau surrounding the Craven's House which was located about halfway up the mountain. A fog had shrouded the slopes of

Lookout most of the morning, becoming very heavy by
2:00 P.M. This "cloud" worked to the Federal's advantage,
hiding much of their movements from the Rebel forces
defending the mountain, and effecting several "surprises"
upon the enemy. Their audience of 30,000 Federals,
watching anxiously from the valley below, could see
nothing, although the roar of battle could be heard on
Orchard Knob four miles away. Their anxiety is expressed
in a letter written by Major James A. Connolly to his wife.[*]

*Away off on our right—three miles away on the
opposite side of Lookout—we hear firing. What can that
mean? Suddenly the cannon with which we have been
pounding away at Mission Ridge are silent and all eyes are
turned westward toward Lookout Mountain. The sounds of
battle increase there, but it is on the other side of the
mountain from us and we can see nothing, but the word
passes around: "Hooker is storming Lookout!" My heart
grows faint. Poor Hooker with his Potomac boys are to be
the forlorn hope! What? Storm that mountain peak 2,400
feet high, so steep that a squirrel could scarcely climb it,
and bristling all over with Rebels, bayonets and cannon?
Poor boys. Far from your quiet New England homes, you
have come a long way only to meet defeat on that mountain
peak, and find your graves on its rugged sides. Lookout
Mountain will only hereafter be known as a monument to a
whole Corps of gallant New Englanders who died there for
their country.*

---

[*] Connolly, who fought three years in the Army of the Cumberland, was a leading Civil War Diarist.

Along with Hooker's New England boys storming the mountain were Whitaker's Midwestern troops from Indiana, Ohio, Kentucky, and Illinois. Henry describes the action of these regiments:

The upper slope and northern end of Lookout were now assailed by a fierce artillery fire from batteries in Lookout Valley and from Moccasin Point. A number of commanding hills now took an interest in the topography of Lookout and began to drop shells in advance of our lines in places where they were likely to do the most good for us. And over the shoulder of Lookout we could hear Brannon's* guns defying their old antagonist with a fury that boded no good to any within the range of his guns. The Rebel batteries on the side of the mountain swept the slope along and up which our forces were making their toilsome advance, and the high perched batteries on the crest of the mountain sent their iron hail both right and left, but far over my brigade as they could not depress their guns sufficiently to bare on us.

---

* Brannon's regiment was hidden in the woods at Chickamauga, causing Rosecrans to think there was a gap in the line. He was among those forces left with Thomas at Horseshoe Ridge when Rosecrans fled the field.

The Rocky sounding board on our right tossed back the report of our own guns. It seemed to be a continuous roar and the guns over our heads made it seem as though the entire vault of the sky had exploded with each retort.

The artillery fire quickened our advance and we soon reached the downward slope to the left and toward the Craven House where we took a few prisoners. Soon we came in sight of the Rebel works below and in front of us. To the right of us were two cannon a-pounding away at Hooker's men. But first, then and there, we, the 96th Illinois, the 40th Ohio, and 8th Kentucky, made a discovery that made us feel better than would a whole box of Hardtack. That was the construction of the Rebel works. They faced the other way and so did the Jonnies that filled them!—their guns all pointing down the mountain instead of up!

We took in the situation at once. I don't say whether there was an order to charge or not, but charge we did and such a charge! It was the first foot of ground that we had found yet that we could make good time over, and we got there, but how! Some rolled, some tumbled, some slid. Some of the Rebs that we took in said they were a watching for Yanks in front and did not think there were any Yanks behind them. But when they heard our yell—for yell we did—and looked around and saw the whole upper side of the mountain covered with Yanks a-coming through the air (ass)* first at them, it was time to quit. So they threw down their arms and pled for mercy.

But the 40th Ohio went too far and a Rebel force got between them and us on our right. We sent our prisoners to the rear, something over 300. We then began a right flank movement, starting to swing around Point Lookout, the right of our regiment being the pivot and the left of the line sweeping around toward Chattanooga.

Is it too much to say that the Clock of History struck high noon when that mighty Index Finger pointed due north on that rocky Dial Face? Certainly the afternoon of the Confederacy began to decline from that hour. Our charge on the entrenchment was like an avalanche. The enemy retreated along the mountainside toward the Craven House leaving many prisoners in our hands. The fog

---

* Henry has made a little drawing of the animal, for he is too much the gentleman to use the word.

was very dense where we were and up above us, but it rained below us which was a perplexity to us and yet salvation for us. While it bothered us in keeping our alignment, it also prevented the Reb minions from the crest of Lookout drawing a bead on us. This battle has been called the "Battle Above the Clouds," but really, it was a battle in the clouds."

At twelve o'clock our alignment was complete. We had helped the 40th Ohio out of their tight place and in doing so, had captured two pieces of ordinance.

A little after 1:00 P.M. Whitaker and a portion of his staff had possession of the Craven House from which they sent messages at 2:00 to Generals Cruft, Granger, and Thomas announcing their success. Whitaker did not see or know of the order sent to Cruft's command from General Hooker directing "that as soon as the enemy are started, our forces pursue to the crest of Lookout slope only, there the lines will be formed. Pursue no further than the rest until further orders..." By the time Whitaker received this directive, via General Grose late in the evening, his command had already driven the enemy nearly three-quarters of a mile beyond the crest of Lookout slope.

With momentum born of success, the 96th Illinois and 40th Ohio went into action again. According to Henry:

The 96th again swang to the right and the 40th Ohio advanced across on open space and aligned on the 96th. We then advanced to the old rail fence. From this point the battle raged with renewed vigor. We continued to drive the enemy towards the eastern slope and towards the Summertown Road, a road which the Rebs wanted very much to hold, so their lower lines were reinforced by General Jackson's Division of Mississippi and Georgia troops. The battle raged hot and heavy until two o-clock. Jackson's men took a very strong position south of the Craven House to protect the Summertown Road, their only road of escape from the mountaintop. At this time our ammunition was expended.

The 96th Illinois had had 29 men wounded and one man killed. The wounded had left their ammunition with us, but we were in no condition after our rough and tumble climb over the rocks, through the brush and felled timbers, down through ravines filled with briars and bramble which we had to lay hold of to pull ourselves up the steep sides. I say we were in no condition to attack the Rebel hoards in front of us by main strength and bayonets alone.

About this time the clouds lifted, the wind sprang up, and we could begin to see something of our surroundings. We soon heard from below a great noisy shouting and cheering. Bands playing. Drums beating. The army near Chattanooga had got a glimpse of the Army Above the Clouds.

Major Connolly had been keeping vigil along with the rest of the Union Army in the valley that day. Anxiously scanning the mountain with his glass, he saw a straggler from time to time and heard the sounds of battle. He described the awful wait in a letter to his wife.

Minutes drag like hours, the suspense is awful, but look! Here comes a crowd of stragglers! Here they come by hundreds, yes by thousands! The mountain is covered with them! They are broken, running! There comes our flag around the point of the mountain! There comes one of our regiments on the double quick! Oh! Such a cheer as then went up in the valley! Many cheeks were wet with tears of joy, our bands played "Hail To The Chief," and 50 brazen throated cannon, in the very wantonness of joy thundered out from the fortifications of Chattanooga, a salute to the old flag which was then on the mountaintop. The work was done. Lookout was ours, never again to be used as a perch by Rebel vultures. Didn't we of the old Army of the Cumberland feel proud though? It was one of the regiments that fought at Chickamauga that carried that first flag to the mountaintop. It was a brigade of the old Chickamauga army that led the storming party up the mountain.

With the lifting of the fog, Henry assessed their situation:

Hooker had made a clean sweep at the base of the mountain so that we were reinforced from the Army of the Cumberland, they bringing ammunition on their persons and on horseback. After this, the fighting was confined to a ratting and brisk skirmish fire for the rest of the afternoon and well into the evening. At about ten or half past ten o'clock, our hair was started up by hearing the Rebel yell and a ratting volley of musketry that proved to be a feint to cover their retreat from the top of the mountain. We kept in battle line and lay on our arms until daylight.

On the morning of the 25th the sky was perfectly clear, not a cloud to be seen. I think our first look was up to scan the crest of Old Lookout, and looking for the muzzle end of Rebel muskets. We also listened for some sound of a warlike nature, but none were heard. Soon General Walter Whitaker was heard calling for volunteers to scale the dizzy height and place the flag on the top of old Lookout. The 96th Illinois lay close up to the Palisade and was first called on, but Colonel Champion told the General we had no flag staff and not much left of our flag, it having been all shot to pieces at Chickamauga. So the General, being a Kentuckyen with pardonable pride, called on the 8th Kentucky, they having had a new flag,* and fifteen men stepped out from that regiment and were joined by a half dozen from our regiment.

We climbed through the crevices of rock and with the help of poles gained the summit. Soon the flag of the Union was given to the breeze, and proclaimed to the armies at Chattanooga and in the valleys below that our rough and tumble fighting in the clouds had not been in vain. It had made it possible for our armies to operate in the valley below, and toward Rossville, and Mission Ridge, as they could not do while the Rebels held that lofty position on Lookout.

But this was not altogether a bloodless battle on either side as may be gathered from reports of the 24th Mississippi Rebel colonel: 356 men and officers in line of which 199 were killed or wounded that day. The loss in our brigade was quite considerable, the 40th Ohio losing Major Acton who was killed south of the Craven House. The 96th lost one killed,

---

* "This flag was the gift of the loyal women of Estill County, Kentucky. It has been most honorably borne." (Whitaker)

and 19 wounded. I have their names at home.

General Whitaker reported 500 prisoners taken by his command. "My loss in killed is one officer and 16 enlisted men. Wounded: 6 officers and 52 enlisted men. Two were missing, making an aggregate loss of 82 men." His loss of 5-1/2% was considerably less than the 55% loss he suffered at Chickamauga. He concludes in his report:

Our country, his family, and his friends have to mourn the loss of Major Acton of the 40th Ohio. He was among the best officers in the service. It is a source of great satisfaction to have been instrumental in accomplishing such magnificent and important results with so little loss, and I can only attribute it to the care of the Providence who spread the Mantle of His Protection over us; and the bold impetuosity of my brave men that bore down, and gave the enemy no time to rally their broken columns.

Even though the Battle Above the Clouds was a glorious victory for the Union forces, there had been some controversy about its military importance. Henry was very much aware of this.

There has been some dispute among military critics as to whether the rough and tumble fight over the shoulder of Lookout was really a battle or not. Some say that it was striking in spectacular effect, affording abundant material for the poet* and the artist. But if these adverse critics had viewed it from the front line of battle as I did, and had realized the same feelings creeping up their spine and then down to their knees, and in fact, that peculiar feeling in the bowels that makes one stop to think when he took the last dose of castor oil, I think they would believe that there had been a fight.

Well, I will now take you back to the planting of the flag on the top of Lookout by the 8th Kentucky, and it was not long before both regiments, the 8th Kentucky and 96th Illinois were up. Also, we took our breakfast up there which consisted principally of coffee and a little more coffee as our haversacks were mostly empty of hardtack.

We are now on the top of old Lookout and we scout around to see what is there. We find some homemade tents, a large quantity of homespun garments such as shirts and drawers and cotton blankets, probably made by Rebel mothers, sisters, or sweethearts. Also a large quantity of cornbread and biscuit

---

* The Battle Above the Clouds was the subject of much poetry. One of these, published in *The Blue and The Gray: Best Poems of the Civil War,* is signed "T.B." It is included at the end of this account.

made from pea meal and bran which we made good use of as we had not had an issue of rations for five days. We had been on short and poor rations while over the river on Moccasin Point, and in fact no rations at all. But we thought it very tough to have to live on the kind of food that we found up there on the mountain, for it was mixed with mould and corn husks.

It was bitter cold up there. We longed for our knapsacks and blankets which we had left down below, but we could not get them. A fire was a great luxury for the wind would sweep one off the mountain almost as soon as built. Even the tents that we found there could not be kept in position to do us much good, for fasten them the best we could, the wind would soon tear them up, and some of the men were hurt by falling trees, one man having his leg broken.

Chapter Twelve
Act 3: Missionary Ridge, Nov. 25

The third and decisive act of the drama at Chattanooga was enacted in three stages on November 25th. After the humiliating defeat at Chickamauga in September, and near starvation in Chattanooga in October, the glory and excitement of victory at Lookout was just the tonic the Union troops needed to prime them for battle at Missionary Ridge. However, Bragg had concentrated his forces—23 brigades in all—upon this strategic ground and was prepared to hold fast.

At sunrise Sherman renewed his bid for Tunnel Hill at the North end of Missionary Ridge, but the Confederates had spent the night strengthening their position which now formed Bragg's right. By 3:00 P.M. the Army of the Tennessee had made little progress.

Hooker, in the meantime, was also experiencing his share of troubles. Ordered to "intercept the enemy's retreat, if he still remained; if he had gone, then move directly to Rossville and operate against the left rear of the force on Missionary Ridge," he was unable to cross Chattanooga Creek. The Confederates had burned the bridge while escaping from Lookout Mountain. The Army of the Potomac was delayed three hours rebuilding the bridge.[*]

---

[*]" …the 96th did not take part in the Battle of Mission Ridge as did the balance of the brigade, except the 8th Kentucky which was on the mountain with us…" (Henry Annis)

Grant's plan to hit both ends of the Confederate line at once was thwarted.

While the two veteran corps struggled, Thomas, with his unproven Army of the Cumberland, was waiting to move out against the Confederate center on Missionary Ridge. Time was getting late and Grant, realizing Sherman's failure to obtain his objective and Hooker's delay in reaching his, ordered the signal—six cannon fired in succession—for Thomas to attack.

Missionary Ridge is rugged and steep. Rising from 200 to 400 feet, its slopes are dotted with boulders and stumps and broken by ravines. Bragg's first line of defense—half his force—was positioned at the bottom of the hill with secret orders to fire a volley when the enemy was within 200 yard, then retreat up the hill. However, Bragg had a communication problem as well as a cooperation problem. Many of his men were unaware of the secret plan and failed to pull back as instructed.

Bragg's second and final line of defense was to defend and hold the highest ground, which militarily is defined as "the highest place from which you can see and fire upon an approaching enemy." The Confederates mistakenly interpreted this as the highest ground geographically, which they accordingly prepared to defend. This mislocation of lines created "dead spaces" through which their attackers could advance under cover.

Grant had ordered his attacking army to halt after taking the first line and reorganize. Effecting this order would have been suicide, for anyone lingering in this position would be subjected to murderous fire from the crest of the hill. As with the Lookout assault on the previous day, the Union troops ignored the order to halt, and after overwhelming Bragg's men at the base, continued on immediately for the summit.

With cries of "Remember Chickamauga!" Thomas's army raced to the top of the Ridge, throwing caution to the wind as the misdirected Rebel shells burst over their heads and behind them. The regimental colors were passed from bearer to bearer as each competed to be the first to gain the top. Connolly, a participant in this action, wrote: "...the batteries have ceased, for friend and foe are mixed in a surging mass, in a few minutes the flags of 60 Yankee regiments float along Mission Ridge from one end to the other. The enemy are plunging down the eastern slope of the Ridge and our men are in hot pursuit..."

In his Civil War history, *The War Years*, Carl Sandburg observed, "For the first time in a large-scale combat, Confederate soldiers had been routed, had run away."

William Wood, author of *Captains of The Civil War,* described the rout of the Rebels: "Bragg lost all control of his men. Stores, guns and even rifles were abandoned. Thousands of prisoners were taken, and most of the others were scattered in flight. The battle, the whole campaign, and even the war in the Tennessee sector were won."

Henry Annis, viewing the whole panorama from his uncomfortable perch on top of Lookout Mountain, wrote:

I may truthfully say that it was not often the chance for a soldier in the ranks or out, to be out of danger and have such a splendid sight of so grand a movement of so many soldiers moving on almost impregnable works of a brave and determined effort, as when the Union Army moved on Mission Ridge on the 25th of November, 1863. The view that the 96th Illinois and the 8th Kentucky had from the top of the historic mountain may never and probably never will be repeated. May the Powers That Be grant that there will never be a necessity for it.

This was his bird's-eye-witness account.

There had been arrangements going down around Chattanooga and Orchard Knob. The bugle sounded a fall-in and the two regiments had to climb down the rocks and form the rest of the brigade, taking their place in the division army corps. It was a clear bright day. Mission Ridge could be plainly seen and we noticed the officers a-pointing that way, and now and then taking a look with their field glasses.

We wondered what was up, but we soon got orders to go back onto the mountain—that is the 8th Kentucky and 96th Illinois. We stayed there eight days a-fortifying and guarding the mountain. But there was something taking place at Orchard Knob and towards Mission Ridge that took all our attention. We could see from our lofty position the Army of the Cumberland which had formed between us and the Ridge; and the other armies which stretched away to the left and connected with Sherman's Army on the northern end of Mission Ridge. It was the grandest view of our lives.

It is not my intention to give you a description of the Battle of Mission Ridge. Suffice it to say that it was my privilege to stand on the highest part of the crest of Old Lookout and view the two armies in deadly combat, the lines of Bluecoats reaching from Rossville, the south end of Mission Ridge, along the Chattanooga Valley to Orchard Knob, thence stretching away to the Tennessee River at the northern end of the Ridge where Sherman was forcing his way into line with the rest of the army.

When he had gained the proper place, we heard the signal guns, which was six guns discharged in rapid succession. Then we saw that vast army, four miles in length, all moving forward as if on Dress Parade. We looked, and said to our comrades, "Why don't the Rebels shoot?" for we could see the Rebel fortifications on the Ridge with over four score of cannon all pointing towards that (as we supposed) doomed army of Bluecoats. But our brave boys pressed on and on, near and nearer. The Rebels stood looking at them as if transfixed by their presumption.

We hardly breathe, the suspense is so great. But the scene changes. That whole line in battle array from the top of the Ridge are sending forth their leaden hail, and every cannon seems to be dealing out death and destruction from their fiery mouths to the doomed army below. But the too sanguine Jonnies have waited too long. Their shot and shells pass over the heads of the other force and burst far in their rear.

The air is filled with smoke. Our view is partly shut out. We seem to hear a great shout. The wind lifts the smoke. We can see our brave boys a-climbing up the side of Mission Ridge. They gain the breastworks! They are over! We see the Rebs roll back toward the left. We now know that another great battle is won! The victory is ours—all made possible through the taking of Lookout Mountain.

Mark Boatner, author of *The Civil War Dictionary*, evaluated the campaign::

The loss of Chattanooga was a severe blow to the dying Confederate cause. A vital link of lateral communications was lost, and the stage was set for Sherman's move to split the Confederacy further by his Atlanta campaign and march to the sea."

Henry sums up the victory:

Suffice it to say that the battle won for us all that could be expected. It was a terrible defeat to the Rebels and caused them to move back entirely away from Chattanooga with a heavy loss to them in dead, wounded, and prisoners.

---

[*] See Livermore's *Table of Numbers and Losses at Chattanooga*, Appendix E.

Epilogue

What became of the men whose lives had run the same course for a short, but historically significant portion of time?

Ulysses S. Grant rose from near-disgrace in his faltering military career in 1854 to promotion as General-in-Chief of the Armies of the United States on March 12, 1864, taking over strategic direction of the War and accepting the Surrender of the Confederates from General Robert E. Lee at Appomattox Courthouse on April 9, 1865

He rose to even greater heights in civilian life, becoming 18th President of the United States in 1868 for two badly mismanaged terms. Despite high office, perhaps his greatest accomplishment was his two volume honest and straight-forward autobiography, *Personal Memoirs of U.S. Grant*, finished just a few days before he died of throat cancer in 1885 at the age of sixty-three.

Braxton Bragg, the unpopular Confederate general who was described by historian Victor Hicken as a man "whose faults were so few and yet so great that his virtues were overcome by them," became military advisor to Jefferson Davis after being relieved of his command. He was captured by the Union forces in Georgia on May 9th, 1865, and later paroled. Returned to civilian life, he worked as a civil engineer in Texas until his death in 1876 at the age of fifty-nine.

William Rosecrans was the exact antitheses of his counterpart, Bragg. According to Hicken, he was "an extraordinarily popular man with the common private." Resigning from the army in 1867, he served as Minister to Mexico from 1868 to 1889, and was a California Congressman and rancher. "Old Rosey" died in 1898 when he was seventy-nine.

George Thomas, the "Rock of Chickamauga" was one of fifteen officers given the "Thanks of Congress for Franklin and Nashville." He continued his military career in the regular army, dying at the age of fifty-four on active duty while commanding the Military Division of the Pacific in 1870.

General Gordon Granger reached the apogee of his career at Chickamauga for which he was rewarded with the command of the Fourth Army Corps. However, he failed in subsequent actions to live up to the promise shown in that battle. He stayed in the military, dying on active duty as Colonel of the 15th Infantry in 1876 when he was fifty-four.

James Steedman, a printer by trade, had served in the Texas Army and Ohio Legislature before the War. After the War, in 1866, he resigned his commission to again serve in the legislature. Active in public affairs and newspapering during most of his life, he died in 1882 at the age of sixty-six.

Walter C. Whitaker was serving in the State Senate when the Confederates invaded Kentucky. He was responsible for proposing the resolution putting the state within the Union. Unfortunately, "his...marked individuality of manner and character, and …impetuous temper…involved him in numerous personal difficulties, and led to his becoming, for a time, an inmate of an insane asylum. But in his later years he fully recovered his health and had his share of legal practice." Walter Whitaker died in 1887 at the age of sixty-four.[*]

Little is known of Thomas Emmet Champion. The records show that he died in 1873, but no birth date is given.

Henry Brown Annis finished up his military career in the same place he began it—the hospital. His army record lists him as "sick and sent to hospital at Nashville, Tennessee December 16/64," and also "sick in hospital, Pulaski, Tennessee, January and February, March and April 1865." The Civil War ended in April of '65 and Henry was mustered out of the army at Camp Harker, Tennessee June 10, 1865, two months short of his three year enlistment period.

Henry returned to Emma and their three little girls, and the Annis family resumed their westward trek. Their progress can be traced by the birthplaces of their last six children. On April 10th, 1866 Genivieve was born at Lake Mills, Iowa, and a year later, in 1869 another baby girl was born and died at Bristol, Wisconsin. Emma Relief was born May 16, 1871 at Crystal, Wisconsin. By 1873 Henry and Emma apparently found the home they had been seeking. Their last three children were all born in Columbus, Wisconsin—Lettice June on April 18, 1873, and finally,

---

[*] Boatner Page 63.

two boys. Henry Purl, a Centennial baby arrived on December 21, 1876, and over four years later in 1880, twenty-seven years after the birth of their first child, their tenth and last child, my grandfather, Carlton Bruce, made his entrance into the world on the Fourth of July. Henry was forty-nine, Emma forty-five.

As the children grew up, they left home. After first moving to the Minneapolis-St. Paul area, some of them continued their parent's westward trek; Ella to Proctor, Minnesota; Carrie to Huron, South Dakota; Lettie June to Oregon; and Purl to the West Coast. Genieieve died in 1903, her mother, Emma, in 1904 in Columbus. Soon after, Henry joined his children and his brother, Levi,* in the Twin Cities area of Minnesota. Carlton Bruce made the move a few years later.

Even though he had lived the major part of his life in the 19th Century, Henry Annis was a busy part of the 20th. He was 75 when he married the widow, Hannah Lofgren, and like many Civil War veterans of the time, he and Levi spoke at many patriotic events. Henry spent the last years of his ample life in the Old Soldiers' Home, outliving all his commanding officers. He died in 1922, a year after his brother Levi, at the ripe old age of 91.

In St. Anthony Village, a suburb of Minneapolis where Old Highway 8 intersects with St. Anthony Parkway, is an old, but still flourishing cemetery known by the pastoral name of "Hillside." A small, but exclusive section of that

---

* Levi had also fought for the Union in the Civil War: Company A 10th Minnesota Infantry.

hallowed ground has been reserved for Veterans of the Civil War. Henry Annis's bones lie there in the ground under his marker in the shadow of the cannon guarding these graves.

June Irene Anderson

Poem
The Battle Above the Clouds

*By the banks of Chattanooga watching with a soldier's
heed,
In the chilly autumn morning, gallant Grant was on his
steed;
For the foe had climbed above him with the banners of
their band,
And the cannon swept the river from the hills of
Cumberland.*

*Like a trumpet rang his orders: "Howard, Thomas, to the
bridge!
One brigade aboard the Dunbar! Storm the heights of
Mission Ridge.
On the left the ledges, Sherman, charge and hurl the Rebels
down!
Hooker, take the steeps of Lookout and the slopes before
the town!"*

*Fearless, from the northern summits, looked the traitors
where they lay,
On the gleaming Union army, marshaled as for muster-day.
'Til the sudden shout of battle thundered upward its alarms,
And they dropped their idle glasses in a hurried rush to
arms.*

*Then together up the highlands, surely, swiftly, swept the
lines,
And the clang of war above them swelled with loud and
louder signs.
'Til the loyal peaks of Lookout in the tempest seemed to
throb,
And the star-flag of our country waved in smoke on
Orchard Knob.*

*Day and night, and day returning, ceaseless shock and
ceaseless change.
Still the furious mountain conflict burst and burned along
the range,
While with battle's cloud mingled densely mist and rain,
'Til the ascending squadrons vanished from the gazers on
the plain.*

*From the boats upon the river, from the tents upon the
shore,
From the roofs of yonder city anxious eyes the clouds
explore:
But no rift amid the darkness shows them father, brother,
sons,
While they trace the viewless struggle by the echo of the
guns*

*Upward! Charge for God and Country! Up! Aha! They
rush. They rise,
'Til the faithful meet the faithless in the never-clouded
skies.
And the battlefield is bloody where a dew-drop never falls,
For a voice of tearless justice to a tearless vengeance calls.*

And the heaven is wild with shouting: Fiery shot and
bayonet keen
Gleam and glance where freedom's angels battle in the
blue serene.
Charge and volley fiercely follow, and the tumult in the air
Tells of right in mortal grapple with Rebellion's strong
despair.

They have conquered! God's own legions! Well their foes
might be dismayed,
Standing in his mountain temple 'gainst the terrors of his
aid;
And the clouds might fitly echo 'pon loud and parting gun
When from upper light and glory sank the traitor host,
undone.

They have conquered! Through the region where our
brothers plucked the palm,
Rings the noise in which they won it with the sweetness of a
psalm;
And our wounded, sick and dying, hear it in their crowded
wards,
'Til they know our cause is Heaven's and our battle is the
Lord's.

And our famished captive heroes locked in Richmond's prison-hells
List those guns of cloudland booming glad as freedom's morning bells,
Lift their haggard eyes, and panting, with their cheeks against the bars,
Feel God's breath of hope, and see it playing with the Stripes and Stars.

Tories, safe in serpent-treason, startle at those airy cheers,
And that wild, ethereal war-drum, falls like doom upon their ears;
And that rush of cloud-borne armies, rolling back the nation's shame,
Frights them with its sound of judgment and its flash of angry flame.

Widows weeping by their firesides, loyal hearts despondent grown,
Smile to hear their country's triumph from the gate of heaven blown.
And the patriot poor shall wonder, in their simple hearts to know
In the land above the thunder, their embattled champions go.

                                        T.B.

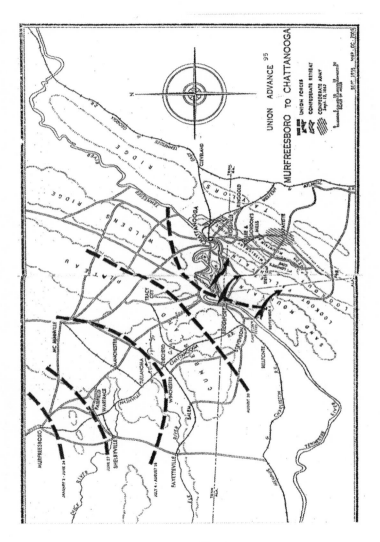

Appendix A

June Irene Anderson

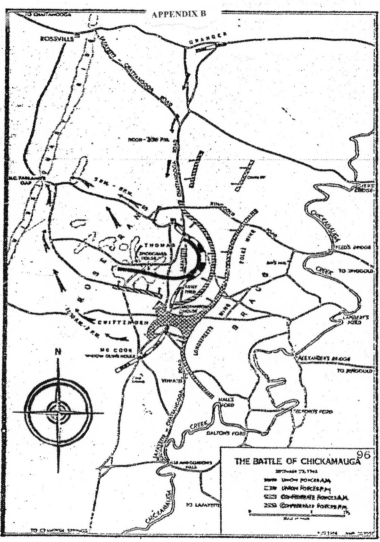

Appendix B

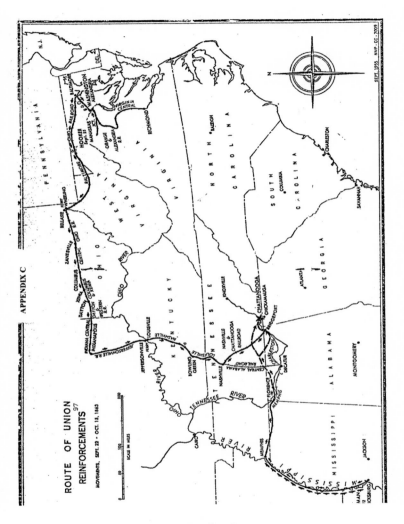

Appendix C

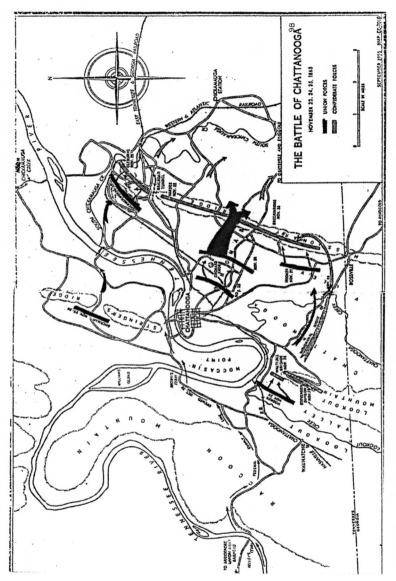

Appendix D

Appendix E

Livermore's Table

Numbers and Losses at Chattanooga Nov. 23-25

	Union	Confederate
Effectives	56,359	64,165
Killed	753	361
Wounded	4,722	2,160
Missing	349	4,146[*]

Livermore's system of comparing relative effectiveness of opposing troops: Federals killed or wounded 44 for every 1000 of their troops engaged. Confederates killed or wounded 118 for every 1000 of their troops engaged.

---

[*] Confederates, thoroughly demoralized and hating Bragg, were suffering a high percentage of desertions at this point of time.

June Irene Anderson

BIBLIOGRAPHY

Primary sources:
Annes, Alonzo L., Compiler. "Form for Insertion of Record in Annis Genealogy." Janesville, Wisc. June 18th 1892.

Annis, Henry. *Official Army Record, Co. B, 96th Regiment Illinois Infantry*, Sept. 5, 1862-June 10, 1865.

Annis, Henry. Unpublished Memoirs, "Our Experience At and On Lookout Mountain, Nov. 24, 1863" circa 1865-1921.

Capps, Claudius Meade. *The Blue and The Gray: The Best Poems of The Civil War*. New York: Books for Libraries Press, 1969.

Commager, Henry Steel, editor. *The Blue and The Gray: The Story of the Civil War as Told by Participants*. Indianapolis: Bobbs-Merrill, 1950.

Connolly, James. *Three Years in The Army of The Cumberland*. Bloomington: Indiana University Press, 1959.

Crozier, Emmet. *Yankee Reporters 1861-65*. New York: Oxford University Press, 1956.

Moore, Frank, editor. *The Rebellion Record: A Diary of American Events*, Vol. 8, New York: D. VanNostrand, Publisher, 1865.

Scott, Robert N. *The War of The Rebellion: A Compilation of the Official Records of the Union and Confederate Armies,* Series I, Vol. XVI, Part II: Vol. XX, Part II; Vol XXX, Part I, III: Vol. XXXI, Part II, III, IV. Washington: Government Printing Office, 1890.

Secondary Sources:
Angle, Paul M. *Tragic Years, 1850-65*. New York: Simon and Schuster. 1950.

Barnard, George N. *Photographic Views of Sherman's Campaign*. New York: Dover Publications, Inc., 1977.

Boatner, Mark Mayo. *The Civil War Dictionary*. New York: Van Rees Press, 1959.

Catton, Bruce. From *Introduction to John Ransom's Diary*. New York: Dell Publishing Co., 1954.

Cole, Arthur Charles. *The Centennial History of Illinois*, Vol. III, *The Era of The Civil War, 1848-1870.* Springfield: 1919.

Draper, John William. *History of the American Civil War,* Vol. III. New York: 1870.

Dyer, Frederick H. *A Compendium of The War of The Rebellion*, Vol. II. New York: Thomas Yoseloff, 1959.

Hicken, Victor. *Illinois In The Civil War*. Urbana & London: University of Illinois Press, 1965.

Jordan, Robert Paul. *The Civil War*. Washington DC: National Geographic, 1969.

Pratt, Fletcher, *The Civil War*. Garden City, N.Y: Doubleday, 1955.

Reeder, Red. *The Southern Generals*. New York: Duell, Sloan and Pearce, 1965.

Sandburg, Carl. *Abraham Lincoln: The War Years*, Vol. II. New York: Harcourt, Brace & Co., 1939.

Sullivan, James. *Chickamauga and Chattanooga Battlefields*. Washington DC: Government Printing Office, 1956.

Tebeau, Charlton W. "Chattanooga," *Encyclopedia Britannica*, 1969.

"Thirty Years Ago," *East Minneapolis Argus*, 1951.

U.S. Research Bureau. *Historical and Biographical Sketch of The Annis Family*. No date.

Wood, William. *Captains of The Civil War*. New Haven: Yale University Press, 1921.

About the Author

Wife of one, mother of four and grandmother of ten; schoolteacher, and writer, June Anderson's passions include genealogy and history. Mrs. Anderson holds degrees in Education, English, and Library Science from the University of Minnesota and the College of St. Catherine. Her part-time employment as a substitute teacher allows her to write monthly features for the arts page of the local newspaper, serve as vice president and membership chairman for the county arts alliance, and write the publicity for the local community theater.

In her never-ending exploration of the roots and branches of the family tree, Mrs. Anderson discovered that her fourth cousin's great-grandfather, General Thomas C. Hindman (Confederate) and her own great-grandfather, Private Henry B. Annis (Union) faced-off in the same battle at Chickamauga. "Knowing your roots and finding the relationships and coincidences is what brings history alive," she maintains.

CPSIA information can be obtained at www.ICGtesting.com
Printed in the USA
266280BV00001B/39/A